Preserving the History of Newberrytown is a group dedicated to preserving, collecting, researching, and interpreting historical information or items north of the Conewago Creek.

D1522710

Table of Contents

Thank you

All of the recipes shared in this cookbook have been submitted by residents of Newberry Township and its surrounding areas (past and present). I would like to thank the community for enthusiastically embracing this project and sharing their treasured family recipes with me.

I hope this cookbook will inspire another generation of Newberry Township residents to connect with their family history and keep local traditions alive through food.

- Dominish Marie Miller
Founder of *Preserving the History of Newberrytown*

Follow us on Facebook: Preserving the History of Newberrytown
Follow us on Instagram: @NewberrytownHistory
Follow us on Twitter: @NewberryHistory
Website: https://www.preservingnewberrytown.org/
Email: history@preservingnewberrtown.org

A Happy Home: Submitted by Kyle Bissel. This recipe came from the Wesley and Annie Beard family cookbook.

Ingredients:

4 cups of love
2 cups of loyalty
3 cups of forgiveness
5 spoons of hope
4 spoons of tenderness
4 quarts of faith
1 barrel of laughter

Instructions:

Take love and loyalty, mix thoroughly with faith. Blend it with tenderness, kindness, and understanding.

Add friendship and hope. Sprinkle abundantly with laughter.

Bake it with sunshine, serve daily with generous helpings. (Serve this to your family soon and they will be glad you did).

Anonymous

Condiments

con·di·ment
/ˈkändəmənt/
Noun

Something used to enhance the flavor of food.

Molasses: Submitted by Diane Garman. This recipe belonged to her mother-in-law, Ellen Wilt Garman.

Ingredients:

2 cups sugar
1 cup water
½ teaspoon maple flavoring
½ teaspoon vanilla
Pinch of salt

Instructions:

Bring sugar and water to a boil. Boil for 1 minute.

Lower heat, cover, and cook for 5 minutes.

Add maple, vanilla, and salt.

Homemade Ketchup: Submitted by Kyle Beissel. This recipe belongs to the Beard family.

Ingredients:

½ heaping bushel of tomatoes
2 green peppers
1 tablespoon celery seed
1 large onion
½ teaspoon allspice
3-6 cups of sugar to taste
1 tablespoon salt
1 teaspoon cinnamon

Instructions:

Cook tomatoes, onions, and peppers until soft.

Sieve and add all other ingredients.

Boil until thick, then bottle, and cap.

Apple Peach Jelly: Submitted by Donna Smith

Ingredients:

2 cups apple, chopped (Use tart, unpeeled apples)
2 cups peaches, chopped (Use firm, ripe peaches)
Juice of 2 lemons
3 cups sugar

Instructions:

Cut apples and peaches into small pieces. Combine with lemon juice and sugar.

Cook slowly until the apples are transparent, about 25 mins.

Pour into sterilized glasses and seal.

*Note: Follow canning jelly guidelines.

Meemaw's Cranberry Sauce: Submitted by Harold Hartman

Ingredients:

2 12oz bags of fresh cranberries
1 ¼ cups water
2 cups sugar
1 cup celery, finely diced
1 cup pecans, chopped
1 large apple, diced
1 ½ tablespoons vanilla

Instructions:

Rinse cranberries and put them into a pot with water and bring to a boil.

After cranberries pop and become soft, add sugar and cook for 3 minutes.

Run the mixture through a food mill or ricer.

Add remainder of ingredients and stir.

Cool before serving.

Mixed Pickle (Chow Chow): Submitted by Justin Bartolette. This recipe belonged to his great-grandmother, Ellen Poet.

Ingredients:

1 large head of cauliflower, chopped
1-quart lima beans
1-quart green beans, chopped
2 red peppers, chopped
1-quart carrots, diced
1 bunch celery, diced
1-quart lime pickles, diced
1-quart white vinegar
1 pint of water
6 cups sugar
2 tablespoons salt
1 tablespoon whole cloves
2 cinnamon sticks

Instructions:

Cook each vegetable separately until medium-firm (not soft).

Divide spices into two spice bags.

Heat vinegar, water, sugar, and salt to make a syrup.

Divide vegetables, spice bags, and syrup into two large pots.

Bring to a boil.

Remove spice bags.

Pack the Chow Chow in sterile pint jars, leaving ½ inch of headspace.

Process for 10 minutes in a boiling water-bath canner.

Watermelon Salsa: Submitted by Debbie Sorenson

Ingredients:

2 cups seedless watermelon, diced
¾ cup sweet onion, finely chopped
1 can black beans, drained and rinsed
1 jalapeno pepper, seeded and chopped fine
¼ cup fresh cilantro, chopped
2 tablespoons brown sugar
1 clove garlic, minced
½ teaspoon salt

Instructions:

Combine all ingredients, cover, and refrigerate for at least one hour.

Drain before serving.

India Relish: Submitted by Lana Fink. This recipe is from a 1927 Grange cookbook.

Ingredients:

One-peck green tomatoes
1 medium-sized cabbage
6 onions
3 red peppers
2 green peppers
8 cups sugar
2 tablespoons celery seed
2 tablespoons coriander seed
1 stick cinnamon
1 tablespoon whole cloves
1 ½ cups salt
3 quarts vinegar

Instructions:

Grind the tomatoes, onion, and peppers in a food processor.

Salt and let stand overnight.

Grind cabbage in the morning and add to kettle. Boil for 20 minutes, then add spices, sugar, and vinegar. Boil until tender.

Put cloves and cinnamon in a cloth bag.

Can in pint jars.

"This is so good. I use it in tuna salad and ham salad. My sister eats it on boiled pot pie and hot dogs". - Lana Fink

Cooked Salad Dressing for Macaroni and Potato Salad:

Submitted by Donna Smith. This recipe belonged to her mother and her grandmother.

Boil potatoes or macaroni desired for your salad. Drain and set aside.

Beat together-

6 Eggs

1 cup Sugar

Add-

3/4 cup Water

3/4 cup Vinegar

Cook and stir until it reaches the boiling point.

Remove from heat.

Add-

1 to 2 tablespoons mustard

1/2 to 3/4 cup mayonnaise

Mixing well, pour over your macaroni or potato mixture.

Add-

Chopped hard-boiled egg to top and serve.

Dressing for Potato or Macaroni Salad: Submitted by Debbie Sorenson. This recipe belonged to Grandma Hackenberg.

Ingredients:

2 tablespoons of butter
1 tablespoon of flour
1 cup sugar
1 egg
½ cup cider vinegar
½ cup water
1 tablespoon yellow mustard
3 tablespoons Miracle Whip (heaping)

Instructions:

Melt butter in a saucepan over low heat, slowly whisk in flour and continue cooking for a minute or 2 until you have a thick roux.

Add water, vinegar, sugar, and egg and cook until slightly thick.

Remove from heat and add the mustard and Miracle Whip.

Crock-Pot Meat Sauce: Submitted by Cindy Lawyer

Ingredients:

¾ cup grated or finely chopped onion
1 - 32 ounce bottle of ketchup
½ of the ketchup bottle of water
½ cup sugar
2 tablespoons Worcestershire sauce
2 tablespoons vinegar
2 teaspoons mustard
½ teaspoon garlic powder
½ teaspoon onion powder
Salt and pepper

Instructions:

Mix all together and heat in a crockpot.

Add your choice of cooked meat

My family's favorites are burgers or boneless skinless chicken breasts.

Appetizers

ap·pe·tiz·er
/ˈapəˌtīzər/
Noun

A small dish of food or a drink taken before a meal or the main course of a meal to stimulate one's appetite.

Side Dishes

side dish
/ˈsīd ˌdiSH/
Noun

A dish served as a subsidiary to the main one.

Bread and Butter Pickles: Submitted by Gail Miller. This recipe belonged to her grandmother, Hazel Yinger Erney.

Ingredients:

8 cups sliced cucumbers
2 cups onions, chopped
2 cups vinegar
3 cups sugar
1 ½ tablespoon celery seeds
5 green peppers, chopped

Instructions:

Sprinkle with salt

Boil until soft

Red Beet Eggs: Submitted by Rosie Coligan Helbus

Ingredients:

1 dozen eggs, hard-boiled and shelled
1 jar of beets
1 cup of sugar
1 cup of apple cider vinegar

Instructions:

In a saucepan add beets, sugar, and apple cider vinegar. Heat thoroughly.

Pour over eggs.

Chill in the fridge for 1-2 days.

Pickled Eggs: Submitted by Debbie Sorenson

Ingredients:

2 dozen eggs, hard-cooked and peeled
3 cans of red beets, any cut, with juice
1 ½ Cups cider vinegar
1 ½ Cups sugar
1 teaspoons salt
1 teaspoon whole cloves (optional)

Instructions:

Place peeled hard-cooked eggs in a gallon glass jar. In a large saucepan combine

beets, vinegar, sugar, salt, and cloves. Heat until hot and all sugar has dissolved.

Remove from heat and pour the hot liquid over eggs. Let stand at least 48 hours

before serving. Turn eggs several times to allow the flavor to penetrate properly.

Deviled Eggs: Submitted by Rosie Coligan Helbus

Ingredients:

1 dozen eggs, hard-boiled and shelled
Egg yolks (reserved from hard-boiled eggs)
Mayonnaise, to taste
1 ½ teaspoon yellow mustard
Salt, to taste
Pepper, to taste
Paprika, to taste

Instructions:

Cut eggs in half lengthwise and pop out the yolks.

Mash the yolks (a hand masher works well). Mix with mayonnaise until the mixture is creamy. Add 1 ½ teaspoon yellow mustard. Salt and pepper to taste.

Use a teaspoon to put the egg yolks back into the whites of the eggs.

Sprinkle eggs with paprika.

Hot Jalapeno Crab Dip: Submitted by J. Scott Basslayer

Ingredients:

1 pound crab, flaked
1 teaspoon chopped garlic
½ cup chopped jalapenos
¼ pound Monterey jack cheese, grated
1 teaspoon Worcestershire sauce
½ cup mayonnaise
2-4 ounces of Parmigiano cheese

Instructions:

Mix ingredients.

Bake at 350° F for 25 minutes.

Sprinkle more cheese on top when done and serve on a toasted baguette.

Hoagie Dip: Submitted by Judi Bourque

Dice the following meats, cheese, and veggies:

¼ pound pepperoni
¼ pound Genoa salami
¼ pound deli ham
¼ pound turkey
6 slices provolone
½ diced sweet onion
½ cup banana peppers

Gather:

1 tablespoon banana pepper juice
½ cup mayonnaise
1 tablespoon olive oil
1 tablespoon submarine sauce
1 tablespoon Italian seasoning
1 large tomato- diced
3-4 cups finely chopped romaine lettuce

Mix all together

Serve with pita chips. Can also be used as a sandwich spread.

Baked Corn: Submitted by Rosie Coligan Helbus

Ingredients:

6 tablespoons of flour, heaped high

¼ cup butter, softened

⅓ cup sugar

½ teaspoon salt

1 can whole kernel corn, drained

1 can creamed corn

2 cups milk

Instructions:

Beat flour and eggs together until smooth.

Add butter, sugar, and salt.

Continue beating until well blended.

Stir in corn.

Add milk and blend well.

Bake at 350° F until thickened and slightly browned, 45 minutes to an hour.

An extra can of corn can be added without increasing other ingredients.

Bake uncovered.

Beer Bread: Submitted by Brenda Wylie

Ingredients:

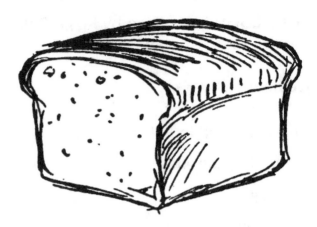

3 cups self-rising flour
3 tablespoons sugar
12-ounce beer

Instructions:

Mix and pour into a greased loaf pan.

Bake at 350° F for 1 hour - 1 hour 15 minutes.

Biscuits: Submitted by Dominish Miller. This recipe belonged to her uncle, Grady Collins.

Ingredients:

2 cups self-rising flour
¼ cup Crisco
⅔ cup milk
Dash of sugar

Instructions:

Place flour and sugar in a bowl.

Add Crisco and cut it in with the flour (until it is coarse like cornmeal).

Pour in milk and stir until batter pulls away from the sides of the bowl.

Flour a piece of tinfoil and place dough on it.

Knead the dough for about 10 minutes and press out like pizza dough.

Cut with a small glass and place on a cookie sheet.

Place in a preheated oven and bake at 450° F for 8-10 minutes or until light brown.

Pineapple Bread Pudding: Submitted by JoAnn Seker

Ingredients:

1 can crushed pineapple
4 cups bread cubes
½ cup butter
1 ⅓ cup sugar
3 eggs, beaten
½ cup milk

Instructions:

Cream butter and sugar.

Add eggs, stir in bread cubes and pineapple.

Add milk.

Pour into a casserole dish and bake for 1 hour at 350° F

Potato Salad: Submitted by Gina Mickle Reever. This recipe belonged to her grandmother, Loretta Harlacher, née Mikos.

Mix:

3/4 cup granulated sugar
1 tsp. salt
2 tablespoons cornstarch
1 teaspoon yellow mustard
2 eggs

Add:

½ cup milk
½ cup cider vinegar

Mix well. Cook and stir constantly over medium to medium-high heat until thick and bubbly.

Remove from heat and add 2-3 heaping tablespoons of Hellmann's mayonnaise and a heaping tablespoon of margarine.

Pour over diced potatoes (cooked soft), chopped celery, and diced hard-boiled eggs.

Clark's Potato Salad: Submitted by Dominish Miller. This recipe belonged to her step-grandfather, Russell Clark.

Sauce: (According to taste)

Mayonnaise
Mustard (French)
Apple Cider vinegar
Water
Sugar (to taste)

Bring to a boil while preparing potatoes.

Boil and cut white potatoes and hard-boiled eggs.

Chop celery, onions, and some carrots. Mix, then add the sauce.

Add salt and pepper to taste.

Serve hot or cold.

Grandma Reinhard's Cucumber Salad: Submitted by Harold Hartman

Ingredients:

Fresh cucumbers
Sweet onion
Salt
Equal parts sugar, Apple Cider vinegar, and water (½ cup of each)
Dill (optional)

Instructions:

Thinly slice cucumbers, ⅛ inch. Thinly slice onions as thin as possible.

Layer sliced cucumbers and onions into a bowl and salt each layer. Use a plate and a weight to press down on the cucumbers and onions. Let salted cucumbers and onions set overnight in the refrigerator.

The next day- drain all of the saltwater off of the cucumbers and onions. Mix with sugar, vinegar, and water thoroughly until all the sugar is dissolved.

Cover cucumbers and onions with sweet and sour dressing. If the dressing doesn't cover the cucumbers, make more. Add dill (optional).

Let marinate for at least several hours. Overnight is even better.

Cheese Log: Submitted by Cindy Lawyer

Ingredients:

8 ounces of cream cheese (room temperature)
8 ounces of grated orange cheddar cheese
½ cup parmesan cheese
¼ teaspoon paprika
¼ teaspoon garlic powder
¼ teaspoon onion powder
1 tablespoon lemon juice
Parsley flakes (fresh or dried)

Instructions:

Mix all ingredients.

Roll into a ball or log shape.

Sprinkle with paprika and roll in parsley flakes.

Stores* well when rolled up in Saran Wrap until ready for use.

Serve with crackers, pretzels, etc.

Meals

meal
/mēl/
Noun

Any of the regular occasions in a day when a reasonably large amount of food is eaten, such as breakfast, lunch, or dinner.

Pancakes: Submitted by Diane Garman. This recipe belonged to her mother-in-law, Ellen Wilt Garman.

Ingredients:

1 heaping tablespoon of baking powder
¼ teaspoon salt
1 tablespoon sugar
1 egg
¾ cup milk + 1-2 tablespoons
1 tablespoon melted butter
1 cup flour

Instructions:

Mix ingredients and ladle onto a frying pan.

Yields 8-10 pancakes

Creamed Dried Beef: Submitted by Gloria Apple

Ingredients:

4-6 ounces chipped dried beef, torn into small pieces
1 small onion, diced
4 tablespoons butter
4 tablespoons flour
2 cups milk
Pepper, to taste

Instructions:

Sauté onions in butter. Add dried beef. Add flour and stir, coating dried beef.

Add milk and stir until the mixture thickens.

Serve over toast, English Muffins, noodles, or potatoes.

*For variety, consider adding 1 cup of shredded cheese, and/or corn, peas, or other vegetables.

Corn Pone: Submitted by Kyle Beissel. This recipe belonged to Katie Heilman.

Ingredients:

1 ½ cups flour
1 ½ cups milk
1 teaspoon baking powder
Pinch of salt
1 ½ cups cornmeal
1 egg, beaten
¼ cup sugar
½ cup soft lard or shortening

Instructions:

Combine lard and sugar, add egg and dry ingredients, then beat in milk, batter should be slightly lumpy.

(Don't over-beat to make corn pone though).

Cook at 400°F for 25 minutes.

Scrapple: Submitted by Kyle Beissel. This recipe belonged to the Beard family.

Ingredients:

½ pound fresh lean pork
2 quarts water
1 ½ teaspoons salt
¼ teaspoon pepper
½ cup yellow cornmeal

Instructions:

Simmer pork in water until very tender in a covered 3-quart pan. Let cool.

Skim fat from the surface of the liquid. Remove meat and chop medium-fine. Save broth. Combine 2 ½ cups strained broth with chopped meat, add seasonings, and cornmeal, and cook, stirring until thickened.

Transfer to a double boiler and cook over simmering water, about 1 hour.

Pour into a buttered bread pan and chill.

Slice about ½ thick.

Brown slices in a hot skillet with butter or bacon fat and serve.

Make a large quantity and it will keep in the refrigerator for several weeks.

One Dish Breakfast: Submitted by Gloria Hoover

Ingredients:

1 large package Ore-Ida frozen potatoes or hash brown potatoes
2 ½ cups milk
1 pound sausage, ham, or bacon (cooked)
6 eggs well beaten
½ teaspoon salt
1 ½ cup grated cheese

Instructions:

Spray a 9 x 13-inch casserole dish.

Put potatoes and meat in the casserole dish.

Beat eggs, salt, and milk together well.

Pour over potatoes and meat.

Top with cheese.

Refrigerate overnight.

Bake at 325° F for 45 minutes.

Baked Oatmeal: Submitted by JoAnn Seker

Ingredients:

3 cups quick-cooking oats
3 cups packed brown sugar
2 teaspoons baking powder
3 teaspoons salt
1 teaspoon ground cinnamon
2 large eggs
1 cup whole milk
½ cup butter, melted
Additional milk

Instructions:

Preheat the oven to 350° F.

In a large bowl combine oats, brown sugar, baking powder, salt, and cinnamon.

In another bowl, whisk eggs, milk, and butter.

Stir into oat mixture until blended.

Spoon into a greased 9-inch square baking pan.

Bake for 40-45 minutes or until set.

Serve warm with milk.

Bean Salad: Submitted by Brenda Wylie

Start with:

1 can green beans, drained
1 can kidney beans, drained
1 can yellow (wax) beans, drained
1 green pepper, chopped
1 jar pimentos, chopped
1 small can of mushrooms, drained
1 small onion, chopped

Mix the following and pour over drained/chopped vegetables:

1/2 cup salad oil
2/3 cup vinegar
1 cup sugar
1 teaspoon salt

Summer Fruit Salad: Submitted by Dominish Miller.
This recipe belonged to her uncle, Grady Collins.

Ingredients for salad:

3 medium bananas
1 cup strawberries (cut in half)
1 cup white grapes (cut in half)
3 medium oranges

Instructions:

Slice bananas and place in a bowl, peel oranges, separate them into slices and cover bananas.

Place grapes and strawberries in the bowl.

Cover the bowl and place it in the refrigerator.

Ingredients for sauce:

1 cup sour cream
1 tablespoon orange juice
1 tablespoon honey

Instructions:

Mix and toss with salad.

Make sure all fruit is covered.

Do not put sauce on the salad until ready to serve.

Makes 10 servings.

Hot Lettuce: Submitted by Donna Smith. This recipe belonged to her mother and grandmother.

Tare desired amount of lettuce for a salad. Cook the desired amount of chopped bacon. Set aside.

Beat together-

1 egg

½ cup Sugar

Add-

¼ cup Vinegar

¼ cup water

Cook, stirring the mixture until it comes to a boil.

Pour over torn lettuce and browned bacon pieces.

Garden Lettuce: Submitted by Donna Myers. This recipe belonged to Sylvia Brother Myers.

Ingredients for salad:

Leaf lettuce

Hard-boiled eggs

Ingredients for dressing:

1 5ox can of evaporated milk

¼ cup Apple Cider Vinegar

4 ½ teaspoons white sugar

½ teaspoon salt

⅛ teaspoon ground black pepper

Instructions:

Whisk the evaporated milk, vinegar, sugar, salt, and pepper together in a bowl until the sugar is dissolved.

Chill until ready to serve.

Do not put the dressing onto the lettuce until ready to eat.

Homemade Taco Soup: Submitted by JoAnn Seker

Ingredients:

1 ½ pounds of ground beef or turkey
1 cup diced onion
1 garlic clove, minced
1 - 28 ounce can of diced tomatoes with juice
1 - 15 ounce can black beans with juice
1 - 15 ounce can of corn with juice
1 package of taco seasoning

Instructions:

Brown meat.

Add onion and garlic, cook for 5 minutes.

Add tomatoes, tomato sauce, beans, corn, and taco seasoning.

Stir.

Cook for 30 minutes.

Serve soup with sour cream, shredded cheese, and crumbled tortilla chips.

Ham and Bean Soup: Submitted by Dominish Miller

Ingredients:

1-pound Northern beans

1 ½ pounds ham or large ham bone with meat still attached

½ cup onion, sliced

½ cup celery, chopped

½ cup carrots, sliced

Water

Salt and pepper to taste

Instructions:

Fill a pot with water, bring to a boil over high heat. Make sure ham bone is covered.

Reduce heat, add other ingredients.

Bring back to a boil, then reduce heat, and cook at a simmer for 2- 2 ½ hours. Keep the pot covered.

Remove bone from the pot and cut off any remaining meat from the bone. Add that remaining meat back into the soup.

Chicken Corn Soup: Submitted by Harold Hartman

Ingredients:

1-quart celery, chopped
1-quart onion, chopped
2 quarts frozen or fresh corn
2 quarts cooked chicken from 10 pounds of chicken legs
4 quarts chicken broth from cooking chicken

Instructions:

Sauté onions and celery in some chicken far, add corn, heat, and mix.

Add 4 quarts of warm chicken broth and heat. Add chicken and thoroughly mix. Cook until vegetables are tender.

Using a slotted spoon, fill the quart containers equally. Top each container with the remaining chicken broth.

Makes approximately 7 quarts of soup.

Chicken Corn Soup: Submitted by Dominish Miller

Ingredients:

5 pounds of chicken
1 onion, chopped
½ cup celery, chopped
4 quarts water
6 cups corn (fresh, canned, or frozen)
1 tablespoon parsley
Salt and pepper to taste
*Optional ingredients: 3 hard-boiled eggs, chopped and rivels

Instructions:

Put chicken, onion, and celery in a stockpot and cover with the water. Bring to a boil.

Reduce heat, skim foam, and cook for about 1 hour or until chicken is cooked through.

Remove chicken from the broth. Allow it to cool to touch and cut into smaller pieces.

On medium heat, add corn to the broth and cook for about 5 minutes. Add chicken meat to broth.

Rivels Ingredients:

2 cups flour
1 teaspoon salt
2 large eggs, beaten

*In a small bowl, combine flour and raw egg to make rivels. Mix by hand until the mixture forms crumbs, pea-sized pieces, and smaller. Add extra flour if the dough is too sticky. Slowly add rivels to the boiling soup. Cook for about five minutes. Stir in chopped hard-boiled eggs. Serve hot.

Chicken Corn Soup: Submitted by Theresa Noble

Ingredients for chicken corn soup:

5–6-pound roaster chicken, remove giblets
1 large onion, chopped
3 large stalks of celery, chopped
3 large carrots, peeled and chopped
1-3 cloves garlic, chopped
1 can of cream-style corn
1 can of whole kernel sweet corn

Ingredients for rivels:

1 cup flour
1 egg
Salt to taste

Instructions:

Place vegetables in the bottom of 5–6-quart slow cooker/ crockpot.

Place chicken on top of vegetables. Fill with water until 2 inches below the fill line. Cook on low for 5-6 hours.

Remove chicken from crockpot and separate to cool.

Prepare rivels and spoon a little at a time into the hot soup. Mix rivels into soup. Add both cans of corn and mix.

Once the chicken has cooled enough to touch, debone the chicken and cut it into bite-sized pieces.

Add chicken to soup and enjoy.

Giblets may be added to soup, but don't recommend cooking them inside the chicken.

Hasen-Kucha: Submitted by Justin Bartolette. This recipe belonged to his great-grandmother, Ellen Poet.

Meat-Filling Ingredients:

1 rabbit or ½ roaster chicken
Flour to make gravy
Salt and pepper to taste

Meat-Filling Instructions:

Cook meat in boiling salted water until done. Remove the meat from the bones. Mix the remaining broth with flour, salt, and pepper to create a gravy. Set aside.

Potato-Filling Ingredients:

4 potatoes, boiled and mashed
¾ cup milk
3 tablespoons butter
3 eggs, beaten
1 cup diced onion
¾ bag bread cubes
Salt and pepper to taste

Instructions:

Combine all filling ingredients, mix well. In a buttered 2-quart casserole dish, layer the filling, then the meat, and a little gravy.

Repeat layers.

Bake at 350° F for 45 minutes.

Squirrel Pot Pie: Submitted by Randy Drais

Ingredients:

1 1/2 pounds squirrel meat
1 tablespoon all-purpose flour
2 tablespoons oil plus more as nee
1 large onion
3 stalks celery
2 carrots
1 tablespoon kosher salt
5 cloves garlic
2 cups beef broth
2 cups Guinness beer
1 can 16-ounce chopped tomatoes
1 sprig of fresh rosemary
4 sprigs of fresh thyme
1 handful about 1/4 cup flat-leaf parsley leaves
1 1/2 teaspoons freshly ground black pepper
1 pie crust for a 9-inch pie
1 large egg, optional

Instructions:

Heat an oven to 400°F. Cut the squirrel meat into 1/2-inch pieces. Sprinkle with the flour and toss to coat evenly and thoroughly.

Heat the oil over medium-high heat until it's almost smoking in a large Dutch oven or other heavy-bottomed pot. Working in batches, brown the meat on all sides until lightly browned and allow it to drain on a paper towel.

While the meat browns, chop the onion, carrot, and celery.

When the meat is all browned and out of the pot, add the chopped vegetables to the pot, sprinkle with the salt, and cook, stirring occasionally, until they're translucent and soft, about 5 minutes. While they cook, mince the garlic. Add the garlic and cook until just starting to turn golden, about 2 minutes more.

The recipe continues onto the next page...

Return the meat to the pan, add the broth, Guinness, and tomatoes to the pot. Scrape the bottom of the pan to loosen any browned bits stuck to it. Bring the mixture to a boil.

Meanwhile, chop the rosemary, thyme, and parsley. Once the mixture is boiling, add the herbs and the pepper. Reduce the heat to maintain a steady simmer. Cook, uncovered, until the mixture thickens, about 1 hour.

Pour the squirrel mixture into a 9-inch pie dish and allow it to cool completely.

Gently place the pie shell over the mixture, pinching the edges to seal. Crack the egg into a small bowl and beat with 1 tablespoon water. Brush the egg and water mixture over the pie crust to enhance browning. Cut three 1/2-inch vents at the center of the crust.

Transfer the pie into the oven and bake until the crust is baked through and browned and the filling is bubbling at the edges, 30 to 40 minutes.

Pickled Heart or Tongue: Submitted by Kyle Beissel. This recipe belongs to the Beard Family.

Ingredients:

1 beef tongue or heart
3 cups vinegar
1 cup or less of sugar
4 teaspoons salt

Instructions:

Must rinse the heart or tongue with cold water, helping to remove excess blood and tissue.

Place heart or tongue in a large kettle. Fill with water until the meat is covered by 2 or 3 inches of water.

Heat meat until the water boils. Reduce heat to a simmer and cook for 3 hours or until tender.

Remove meat from the pot and let it cool while you prepare pickling spices.

Then peel off excess fat off the heart or peel excess skin off the tongue and rinse again.

Bring vinegar, sugar, and salt to boil.

Slice meat, then place it in the vinegar broth, (too sour, add water to dilute) and marinate for 24 hours.

Put it in the refrigerator.

Souse or Pickled Pigs' Feet Jelly: Submitted by Kyle Beissel. This recipe belongs to the Beard Family.

Ingredients:

4 pigs' feet, split
12 peppercorns
1 bay leaf
½ teaspoon salt
3 cups cider vinegar
1 sliced onion
6 whole cloves

Instructions:

Put feet into a kettle and cover with water. Cook until tender.

Remove skin and bones, leaving meat in broth, and add remaining ingredients.

Cook for another 2 hours, remove from heat, and cool.

Place in small glass dishes and refrigerate until ready to eat.

Remove the top layer of lard and slice.

Pork BBQ: Submitted by Matt Sowers

Ingredients:

4 pounds of pork loin (trim fat)
PA Dutch Birch Beer
Sauce of your choosing

Instructions:

Poke a few holes all over the pork loin.

Cover half in Birch Beer.

Cook 8 hours on low.

Drain soda and shred.

Top with your favorite sauce.

***Alternate Instructions-**

Pull out at 7 hours, drain soda,
and shred the meat.

Mix in 2 bottles of your favorite sauce.

Put back in on low and cook for another hour.

Cincinnati Chili: Submitted by Judi Bourque

Ingredients:

2 pounds ground beef
3 large onions, chopped
3 cloves garlic, minced
1 - 15 ounce can tomato sauce
1 cup beef broth
2 tablespoons chili powder
2 tablespoons semi-sweet chocolate
2 tablespoons vinegar
2 tablespoons honey
1 tablespoon pumpkin pie spice
1 teaspoon salt
1 teaspoon cumin
½ teaspoon cardamom
1-2 cans kidney beans, rinsed and drained

Instructions:

Cook beef, onions, and garlic.

Add tomato sauce and broth.

Add spices and simmer for ½ hour.

Add beans and cook until heated.

Serve over 6 ounces cooked fettuccine.

Top with shredded cheese.

Slum Casserole. Submitted by Donna Smith

Mix the following ingredients-
4 cups boiling water
3 pounds hamburger
2 green peppers, chopped
2 onions, chopped
2 cloves of garlic

Cook the above mixture until meat is done, about 20 minutes.

Add the following ingredients to the above mixture-

1 can tomatoes (no2)
1 can Hunts Tomato Sauce
1-pound noodles
Salt to taste
Pepper to taste
Chili Powder to taste

Cook ingredients together until the noodles are done.

Add- 2 cans of drained, sliced mushrooms.

Place mixture in a greased casserole dish. Sprinkle the top heavily with grated cheese and parsley.

Bake 350° F for approximately 1 hour.

Macaroni and Cheese: Submitted by Debbie Sorenson

Ingredients:

1 box macaroni
3 T. butter
3 T. flour
1 can of evaporated milk, plus enough whole milk to equal 2 cups
1/2 tsp. salt
16 oz. block extra-sharp yellow cheese
8 oz block extra sharp white cheese
Panko breadcrumbs

Instructions:

Heat oven to 375. Lightly grease 3 or 4-quart baking dish.
Cook macaroni according to package directions, drain and put in greased baking dish.

Shred cheese in a large bowl and set aside.

Melt butter in a deep saucepan. Whisk in flour over medium heat for about 1 minute.

Gradually whisk in the milk, and salt until smooth.
Slowly add cheese and continue whisking until all the cheese is melted.

Pour the cheese mixture over the cooked macaroni. Sprinkle with breadcrumbs. Bake at 375° F for 45 minutes.

Meatloaf: Submitted by Susan Rudy. This recipe belonged to her mom.

Ingredients:
Onions
Green peppers
Celery
Onion salt
Garlic salt
Celery salt
Worcestershire sauce
Mustard
Eggs
Canned milk
Red pepper or chili powder
Pepper
Tomato paste
Catsup
Parsley flakes
Crackers

*Ingredients to taste

No cooking instructions were included with this recipe.

These ingredients can be used in conjunction with your family's meatloaf recipe to give it a different taste.

Salmon Cakes: Submitted by Gail Miller

Makes approximately 4 salmon cakes

Ingredients:

1 - 16 ounce can of Salmon
1 onion, diced
1 tablespoon parsley, diced
Salt and pepper, to taste
1 egg beaten into ¼ cup milk
4 tablespoons butter
Breadcrumbs

Instructions:

Drain salmon. Remove any skin or bones.

Mix salmon, onion, parsley, egg, milk mixture, and salt and pepper in a bowl.

Form into four patties. Cover in breadcrumbs.

Melt butter in a pan and fry patties until golden brown.

Zucchini Crab Cakes: Submitted by Kyle Beissel. This recipe belongs to Shirley Wilt.

Ingredients:

2 cups zucchini, grated, drained, and squeezed

2 eggs

1 tablespoon mayonnaise

1 tablespoon Old Bay seasoning

Instructions:

Squeeze the zucchini many times, then mix everything.

Add breadcrumbs to form cakes.

Deep fry in hot oil.

Fried Cabbage: Submitted by Cindy Shields. This recipe has been handed down by her mother, grandmother, and great-grandmother.

Ingredients:

1 pound of crumbled bacon
Medium-large head of cabbage, rough cut
1 cup sour cream
½ cup cider vinegar *to taste
¼ to ½ cup sugar *to taste
1-2 tablespoons flour

Instructions:

In a large frying pan, fry the bacon. Crumble when cool. Set aside.

Add cut cabbage to bacon grease. Stir occasionally. Cook until cabbage has browned.

In a bowl, whisk sour cream, cider vinegar, sugar, and flour together.

When cabbage is soft, add the sour cream mixture until cabbage is coated. Cook until the mixture thickens.

Add bacon to the mixture and heat for a moment. Serve hot.

Hungarian Cabbage Rolls: Submitted by Judi Bourque.
This recipe belonged to Judi's mom, Elaine Zanzinger.

*This recipe calls for a pressure cooker. Directions are for an old pressure cooker. I use a crockpot and cook on low for 6-8 hours. You can also bake for 1-1 ¼ hours.

Ingredients:

1 pound chopped beef
1 teaspoon salt
¼ teaspoon pepper
2 tablespoons chopped onion
1 cup rice (cooked)
1 egg
1 can of sauerkraut
1 can tomato soup
1 cup water
8 large cabbage leaves

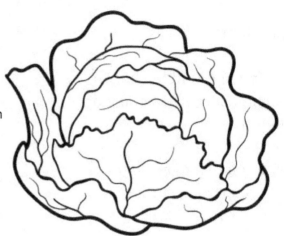

Instructions:

Pour boiling water over cabbage leaves to soften them. Let stand for 5 minutes.

Season meat by adding salt, pepper, onion, rice, and egg. Mix.

Form 8 meatloaves and wrap each in a cabbage leaf. Fasten with a toothpick.

Place cabbage rolls into a pressure cooker. Pour tomato soup, water, and sauerkraut over the rolls.

Cover.
Set the control at 10 and cook for 15 minutes. After control jiggles, let the pressure go down normally.

Serves 4-5 people

Schnitz and Knepp: Submitted by Brenda Fludovich

3-pound piece of ham
1 quart of dried apples

Cover ham with cold water and cook slowly for 2 hours. Add 1-quart dried apples, which have been soaked overnight, and water in which they have been soaking.

Boil for another hour.

Prepare the dumpling batter as follows-

2 cups flour
1 egg
4 teaspoons baking powder
3 teaspoons shortening
1 teaspoon salt
1 teaspoon pepper
1 teaspoon milk

Sift the dry ingredients together; stir in the beaten egg, melted shortening, and enough milk to make a soft batter.

Drop dumplings by the spoonful into the hot liquid, cover the pot tightly, and boil for 20 minutes.

One Dish Chicken and Rice: Submitted by Kathy Witten

Ingredients:

1 can (10 ½ ounces) Campbell's Condensed Cream of Mushroom   Soup
1 cup milk
¾ cup uncooked Minute Rice
Salt, pepper, and paprika for seasoning
4 small chicken breasts or 2 large breasts (boneless, skinless), cut in half lengthwise for thinner pieces

Instructions:

Heat the oven to 375° F. Grease or butter a 9x13 inch baking dish. Combine soup, milk, and rice in a greased baking dish. Season chicken with salt and pepper and sprinkle with paprika. Place the chicken on the rice mixture. Cover the baking dish with aluminum foil.

Bake for 45 minutes or until the chicken is done (time will depend on the thickness of the chicken). Let stand for 10 minutes. Stir rice before serving.

Other Variations:

One-Dish Buffalo Chicken & Rice Bake - Stir 1 cup sliced celery, 1 cup shredded sharp cheddar cheese, and 1 to 2 tablespoons of cayenne pepper sauce into the rice mixture before topping with the chicken.

One-Dish Mexican Chicken & Rice Bake - Reduce the water to ¾ cup. Stir 1 can (about 15 ounces) black beans, rinsed and drained, ½ cup shredded Mexican-blend cheese, and ½ cup Pace Chunky Salsa into the rice mixture before topping with the chicken. After baking, stir the rice and sprinkle with another ½ cup cheese. Cover and let stand for 10 minutes. Sprinkle with 1 tablespoon chopped fresh cilantro leaves, if desired.

Chicken Barbecue and Sauce: Submitted by Deborah Sanders. This recipe belonged to her grandmother, Mrs. Bettie Lentz.

Ingredients:

1 chicken, cut up or just legs, thighs, and breasts
¼ cup melted butter
2 teaspoons salt
½ teaspoon paprika
1 tablespoon sugar
Juice of ½ lemon or 2 tablespoons lemon concentrate
1 teaspoon Worcestershire sauce
1 tablespoon white wine (Famiglia Cribari) or any white wine

Instructions:

Brush chicken with the mixture before placing it on the grill.

Turn and brush chicken several times with mixture during the cooking period.

The cooking time is about 1 hour.

*Can also be cooked in the broiler or the oven.

Hog Maw: Submitted by Cindy Lawyer

Prepare a baking pan with water (up to the first joint on finger - approx. 1 inch).

Ingredients:

3 pounds of potatoes cut into 1-inch cubes
6-8 carrots cut into 1-inch slices
1 medium onion, diced
1 head cabbage, sliced
1 ½ pounds of smoked sausage sliced into 1-inch slices
1 ½ pounds loose country sausage
1 cleaned pig stomach

Instructions:

Mix all ingredients with your hands and stuff them into the pig stomach. It stretches quite a bit. Close end with small skewers or thread.

Place in a pan with water (up to the first joint on finger - approx. 1 inch)

Cover with foil and bake 350° F for 2 ½ hours.

Take off foil and bake for 30-45 minutes longer to crisp the skin.

Let cool for 15 minutes, slice, and enjoy.

Hog Maw: Submitted by Kyle Beissel. This recipe belongs to Dot Wilt.

Ingredients:

1 pig's stomach, cleaned (remove excess fat)
8 potatoes, peeled and cubed
1 pound of loose fresh sausage
1 small head of cabbage, chopped
1 tablespoon salt
Dash of pepper

Instructions:

Mix ingredients. Put into the stomach and sew closed. Excess can be placed in a casserole and baked.

(Oven Browning bag is handy to use). Bake at 350°F until potatoes are soft, about 2 hours.

If no browning bag, place it in a roaster with ¼ cup of water and cover.

Last ½ hour, uncover to brown it.

Homemade Mincemeat: Submitted by Eileen Bink

Ingredients:

5 pounds lean beef or venison, roasted
5 pounds boneless pork, roasted
2 pounds dark raisins
2 pounds white raisins
2 pounds currants
5 pounds Stayman apples (or comparable apples), peeled
4-5 oranges (keep the rind on 1)
3 lemons (keep the rind on 1)
1 tablespoon nutmeg
1 tablespoon Cloves
1 tablespoon Allspice
1 tablespoon Cinnamon
Sugar to taste
1 fifth brandy, whiskey, or rum
1 32 ounces can of Lemon Blend (you can substitute with lemonade)

Put the following together into a 5-gallon crock:

Grind together meats, apples, oranges, and lemons. Stir in raisins and currants. Add sugar, spices, liquor, and lemon drink.

Cover well and keep in a cool spot for about 4-6 weeks, stirring frequently, adding more spices, and liquid as needed (until it "tastes right").

This may be frozen or made into pies or cookies.

Meatballs and Sauce: Submitted by Rosie Coligan Helbus

Ingredients for meatballs:

1 ½ pounds ground beef
1 pound ground Italian sausage
1 egg per pound of meat
1 ½ cups Italian style breadcrumbs
½ cup parmesan cheese

Instructions for meatballs:

Mix thoroughly. Make into golf ball size balls.

Bake at 350°F for 20-25 minutes. Add to sauce when they come out of the oven.

Ingredients for sauce:

1 large onion
6 garlic cloves
Olive oil (enough to cover the bottom of the saucepan)
Basil (1 palm full)
Parsley (2 palms full)
Salt and pepper, to taste
1 small can of 100% natural tomato sauce
1 large can of 100% natural petite diced tomatoes
1 large can of 100% natural crushed tomatoes

Instructions for the sauce:

Build the sauce in layers.

Sauté onions and garlic cloves in olive oil. When translucent, add petite diced tomatoes. When the tomatoes begin steaming, add spices. Mix well.

When this mixture begins steaming, add crushed tomato and tomato sauce. When this mixture begins to boil, lower the temperature to a simmer. The longer you simmer, the better. (Usually a few hours.)

* No oregano in this recipe, "oregano is for pizza sauce".

Seafood Lasagna: Submitted by Cindy Lawyer

Ingredients:

3 green onions, chopped fine
1 bottle clam juice
2 cans clams
2 cans oysters
1 pound crab meat, flaked
1 pound bay scallops
1 pound shrimp, peeled & deveined
½ cup butter + 2 tablespoons, divided
½ cup chicken broth
½ cup flour
1 ½ cup milk
1 cup heavy cream
½ cup parmesan cheese
½ teaspoon salt
Lasagna noodles - oven ready

Instructions:

Sauté onion in 2 tablespoons olive oil and 2 tablespoons butter. Stir in chicken broth and clam juice and bring to a boil. Add seafood. Return to boil. Simmer for 5 minutes. Drain, reserving liquid.

In a saucepan, melt ½ cup butter, stir in flour. Stir the roux until golden brown. Gradually add milk and reserved liquid into the saucepan. Add salt and pepper. Bring to a boil. Cook until liquid thickens, stirring constantly. Turn off heat. Add heavy cream and cheese and stir well. Add ¾ cup of this white sauce to the seafood mixture.

Spread ½ cup white sauce in the bottom of a greased 9x13 inch pan. Place lasagna noodles over sauce. Spread seafood mixture on top of noodles and some white sauce. Repeat layers. Top with cheese. Bake 350° F for 40-45 minutes.

Desserts

des·sert
/dəˈzərt/
Noun

The sweet course eaten at the end of a meal.

Little Dipper Crockpot Fondue: Submitted by Karen Hostetter. This recipe originally belonged to Mary Beth Long and is used at the Red Land Community Library Chocolate Fest.

Ingredients:

1 ½ cups chocolate chips
½ cup heavy cream
1 teaspoon vanilla
*Optional ingredients: 1 teaspoon Bailey's Irish Cream, 1 teaspoon Grand Marnier, 1 teaspoon peppermint, 1 teaspoon rum, 1 teaspoon peppermint schnapps, a pinch of espresso powder

Instructions:

(The portions here fit into a Little Dipper Crockpot. If you do not have a Little Dipper, you can put an oven-safe dish inside of a large crockpot. Do not add water.)

Put chocolate chips into the crockpot.

Add heavy cream and vanilla. Cover.

Cook on low for about 1 hour.

Stir.

Serve with apple chunks, banana slices, cubes of pound cake, strawberries, or marshmallows.

Fudge: Submitted by Connie Anderson. This recipe belonged to her mother and won a Blue Ribbon at the York Fair.

Ingredients:

2 cups sugar
½ cup Carnations Evaporated Milk
1- 12-ounce jar of creamy Skippy peanut butter
1- 7-ounce jar of marshmallow creme

Instructions:

Boil sugar and milk for 3 minutes.

Remove from heat, add butter and marshmallow creme.

Don't beat, but fold until the mixture is smooth.

Place in an 8x8 inch pan or glass dish that has been sprayed with Pam.

Let cool.

*You can add chocolate chips or Hershey's Baking Cocoa for chocolate fudge.

Cut and enjoy!

Peanut Butter Fudge:

Submitted by Susan Rudy.

Ingredients:

4 cups granulated sugar
1 cup canned milk
2 tablespoons white Kayo Syrup
1 tablespoon Apple Cider Vinegar
2 cups marshmallow fluff
2 cups peanut butter

Instructions:

Mix the first 4 ingredients and boil for 4 minutes.

Stir occasionally.

Remove from heat, add peanut butter and marshmallow.

Mom's Peanut Butter Fudge: Submitted by Cindy Lawyer. This recipe belonged to Ardella Wiesner.

Ingredients:

2 cups sugar

½ cup milk

14 ounces of peanut butter

7 ounces of marshmallow creme

Instructions:

Boil the sugar and milk for 3 minutes.

Then add peanut butter and marshmallow creme.

Mix well and pour into a buttered 8x8 inch pan.

Let it set in the refrigerator.

Peanut Butter Fudge: Submitted by Gail Miller. This recipe belonged to her grandmother, Hazel Yinger Erney.

Ingredients:

2 cups sugar
½ cup milk
1 ½ cups peanut butter
1 jar of marshmallow

Instructions:

Bring sugar and milk to a boil. Boil for 3 minutes.

Add peanut butter and marshmallow. Mix well.

Quickly pour into an 8-inch square pan.

Let cool.

Fudge: Submitted by Nancy Heilman Ickes. This recipe belonged to her grandmother, Mary Brenneman Heilman.

Ingredients:

2 cups sugar
1 cup cream or milk
2 tablespoons molasses
1 tablespoon cornstarch
3 tablespoons cocoa
1 tablespoon vanilla
Pad of butter, size of a walnut
3 tablespoons peanut butter

Instructions:

Put all ingredients except for peanut butter into a saucepan.

Boil until it forms a hard ball in cold water.

Beat and add peanut butter (about 3 tablespoons).

Pour into a pan (approximately 8x8 inches).

Cool.

Chocolate Peanut Butter Balls: Submitted by Lou Ann Horvath Kauffman

Ingredients:

1 cup peanut butter
¼ cup margarine or butter, softened
1 cup powdered sugar
2 cups Rice Krispies cereal
1 ½ cup semi-sweet chocolate morsels* see note
2 tablespoons vegetable shortening
54 mini-muffin paper cups

Instructions:

In a large electric mixer bowl, beat peanut butter, margarine, and sugar on medium speed until thoroughly combined. Add Rice Krispies cereal mixing thoroughly. Take a rounded teaspoon of the mixture. Shape into balls. Place each ball in a paper cup. Refrigerate.

Melt chocolate and shortening in a small saucepan over low heat, stirring constantly. Spoon 1 teaspoon melted chocolate over each peanut butter ball. Refrigerate until firm. Store in an airtight container in the refrigerator.

*NOTE: I use Wilbur's Melting Chocolate Wafers and mix about ⅔ dark chocolate and ⅓ milk chocolate. I dip the entire ball into the melted chocolate which I melt in a crockpot. I don't add vegetable shortening.

Butter Taffy: Submitted by Deborah Sanders. This recipe belonged to her grandmother, Bettie Potts, and her great grandmother, Grace Violet Fisher Potts.

Ingredients:

3 cups brown sugar
½ cup molasses
¼ cup hot water
¼ cup vinegar
2 tablespoons butter
1 teaspoon vanilla
Cold water
Black walnuts

Instructions:

Boil brown sugar, molasses, hot water, and vinegar.

When it crisps in cold water, add butter, and vanilla.

Cook for 3 minutes.

Add nuts to the bottom of a buttered pan.

Pour mixture over nuts onto the buttered pan.

Brandied Fruit: Submitted by Donna Smith

In a container*-

Every two weeks add 1 cup of fruit (Pineapple, Peaches, Cherries, etc.), 1 cup of sugar, and stir.

 Serve over ice cream, sponge cake, cottage cheese, etc.

*Never use a TIGHT lid or the mixture will explode.

*DON'T refrigerate the mixture.

Spiced Fruit: Submitted by Donna Smith

Ingredients:

1 can, 1lb 13 oz Peaches or Pears
1/4 cup Apple Cider Vinegar
1/2 teaspoon Whole cloves
1 Cinnamon stick

Instructions:

Drain fruit, reserving the syrup.

Add vinegar, cloves, and cinnamon stick to the fruit syrup. Simmer for 10 minutes.

Add fruit, simmer for 5 more minutes. Cover, and refrigerate overnight to blend the flavors.

Serve chilled as a meat accompaniment or relish tray.

NOTE: Fruit will keep up to a month in the refrigerator. Remove spices at the end of the second week.

Whoopie Pies: Submitted by Donald Resser. This recipe belonged to his mother, Harriet Reeser.

Ingredients for cake:

1 cup Crisco
2 cups sugar
2 egg yolks
1 cup hot water
1 teaspoon baking powder
½ teaspoon salt
4 cups flour
1 cup cocoa

Ingredients (filling):

1 tablespoon vanilla
4 teaspoons flour
1 pound box of 10X sugar
4 teaspoons milk
½ cup butter
1 cup Crisco
2 egg whites

Beat ----

1 cup Crisco
2 cups sugar
2 egg yolks

Add---

1 cup hot water

The recipe is continued on next page…

Sift---

1 teaspoon baking powder
½ teaspoon salt
4 cups flour
1 cup cocoa

Dissolve---

2 teaspoons baking soda in 1 cup sour milk. Add to liquid ingredients.

Add sifted ingredients.

Drop by ½ teaspoons on a baking sheet.

Bake at 350° F for 8 to 10 minutes.

Add filling when the cakes are cool.

Instructions for filling:

Measure out 2 teaspoons 10X sugar. Set the rest of the 10X sugar aside.

Beat together 2 teaspoons of 10X sugar and the rest of the ingredients. --- Add box 10X sugar. Beat until fluffy.

Spread filling between 2 whoopie pies.

Continue until whoopie pies are all filled.

Chocolate/Pumpkin Whoopie Pies: Submitted by Justin Bartolette. This recipe belonged to his great-grandmother, Ellen Poet, and was enjoyed at the annual family Christmas party.

Chocolate Cake Ingredients:

1 cup Crisco
2 cups sugar
2 whole eggs plus 2 yolks
1 cup milk, mixed with 1 tablespoon white vinegar (to make sour)
2 teaspoons vanilla
1 teaspoons baking powder
4 cups flour
1 cup cocoa
½ teaspoon salt
1 cup hot water
2 teaspoons baking soda

Chocolate Cake Instructions:

Cream together Crisco, sugar, eggs, milk, vinegar, and vanilla. Sift flour, cocoa, and baking powder together and stir into batter. Dissolve the baking soda in the hot water and add to the mixture. Drop by the spoonful on a greased cookie sheet. Bake at 400° F for 10 minutes.

Vanilla Filling Ingredients:

2 unbeaten egg whites
2 teaspoons vanilla
4 tablespoons flour
2 teaspoons margarine
1 ½ cups Crisco
1 box 10X powdered sugar

Combine the first 5 ingredients; beat "to death" as Ellen says. Gradually add the box of powdered sugar, beating thoroughly.

The recipe is continued on next page...

Peanut Butter Filling:

Using the above recipe, add ½ - ¾ cup creamy peanut butter to the ingredients and beat well. If the frosting seems too thick, add a little milk.

Cream Cheese Filling:

3 cups 10X powdered sugar
1- 8-ounce bar cream cheese, softened
2 tablespoon margarine, melted
1 teaspoon vanilla

In a large bowl, combine all ingredients, beat until smooth. Add more sugar if the filling isn't thick enough.

Pumpkin Pie Whoopie Pies:

Pumpkin Pie Cake Ingredients:

2 egg yolks
2 cups brown sugar
1 cup vegetable oil
1 teaspoon ground cloves
1 teaspoon cinnamon
1 teaspoon salt
1 teaspoon ginger
1 teaspoon baking soda
1 teaspoon baking powder
1 teaspoon vanilla
2 cups cooked pumpkin
3 cups flour

Pumpkin Pie Cake Instructions:

Beat the egg yolks, brown sugar, and oil together until smooth. Add the pumpkin and dry ingredients. Mix well. Bake at 350° F for 12 minutes. Cool.

Although the vanilla filling can be used for these pies, Ellen suggests using the cream cheese filling instead.

Whoopie Pies: Submitted by Ms. Cook. This recipe belonged to Mabel Markley.

Ingredients:

1 cup Crisco
2 cups sugar
2 eggs + 2 egg yolks
2 teaspoons baking soda
4 cups all-purpose flour
½ teaspoon salt
1 cup sour milk (1 teaspoon vinegar)
1 cup hot water
1 teaspoon baking powder
1 cup cocoa

Instructions:

Cream together sugar, cocoa, shortening, and eggs.

Add sour milk, water, flour, soda, salt, and baking powder.

Mix. "I put baking soda in my sour milk to add it and sift my baking powder in with my flour".

Drop from a soup spoon onto baking sheets.

Allow room for 6 per sheet as they spread.

Bake for 10 - 12 minutes in an oven preheated to 400° F.

When cool, form 2 sandwich cakes.

The recipe is continued on next page…

Whoopie Pie Filling:

2 egg whites
2 teaspoons vanilla
4 tablespoons flour
1 box 10X sugar
1 tablespoon milk
1 ½ cup Crisco

Put all ingredients in one large mixing bowl and mix all at once.

Spread filling between cakes once they are cool.

Peanut Butter Eggs: Submitted by Cindy Lawyer

Ingredients:

2 sticks of butter
2 - 8-ounce packages of cream cheese
2 teaspoons vanilla
36 ounces of creamy peanut butter
2- 2-pound bags of confectioners' sugar
6 cubes of chocolate almond bark
Milk if necessary

Instructions:

Cream together butter, cream cheese, and peanut butter. Then add confectioners' sugar and mix.

If crumbly, add 2 teaspoons of milk. The mixture should mold together easily and not be sticky.

Shape into an egg shape and refrigerate for at least 2 hours.

Melt 6 cubes of chocolate almond bark in a bowl in the microwave until smooth. (Usually for two- 1-minute increments).

Place eggs in chocolate and cover.

Lift with a fork and place on wax paper to dry.

Decorate with colored sugar, sprinkles, or drizzle with white chocolate.

Slice N Spice Cookies: Submitted by Cindy Lawyer. This recipe belonged to Mom Lawyer.

Ingredients:

3 cups of flour
1 teaspoon baking soda
1 teaspoon cream of tartar
½ teaspoon salt
1 cup butter (2 sticks)
2 cups packed brown sugar
2 unbeaten eggs
1 teaspoon vanilla
1 cup of quick-cooking oats
½ cup sugar
4 teaspoons cinnamon

Instructions:

Sift together dry ingredients.

Cream together butter and sugar. Then add eggs and vanilla.

Stir the dry ingredients gradually into the wet ingredients.

Add quick-cooking oats.

Chill for 1 hour in the refrigerator for better handling.

Divide dough into 3 parts on wax paper. Shape into logs.

Wrap with wax paper. Chill for 6-7 hours.

Combine sugar and cinnamon.

Slice log into ¼ inch slices and dip into the sugar mixture (both sides of the cookie).

Bake on a greased cookie sheet at 350° F for 9- 12 minutes.

Grandma's Sugar Cookies: Submitted by Cindy Lawyer

Ingredients:

3 eggs
1 cup butter, softened
2 cups sugar
1 teaspoon vanilla
1 cup sour milk/buttermilk
5 cups flour
1 teaspoon baking soda
2 teaspoons baking powder
¼ teaspoon salt

Instructions:

Make buttermilk: 1 cup milk and 2 tablespoon lemon juice.

Let sit for 30 minutes. (Best to do this first and then gather remaining ingredients).

Cream together eggs, butter, sugar, and vanilla.

Add 1 cup sour milk/buttermilk.

Sift together flour, baking soda, baking powder, and salt.

Add the flour mixture to the wet mixture and mix well. Refrigerate for 1 hour.

Drop by tablespoons onto a cookie sheet or roll out on a floured surface to ¼ inch thickness. Cut out shapes with cookie cutters.

*Decorate with colored sugar, etc.

Bake at 375° F for 8-10 minutes.

Molasses Sugar Cookies: Submitted by Marie Yates

Ingredients:

¾ cup shortening
½ teaspoon cloves
½ teaspoon ginger
½ teaspoon salt
1 cup sugar
2 cups flour
¼ cup molasses
1 teaspoon baking soda
1 teaspoon cinnamon
1 egg

Instructions:

Melt shortening in a 3/4-quart saucepan over low heat.

Remove from the heat and let cool.

Add sugar, molasses, and egg. Beat well.

Sift together all of the dry ingredients and add to the egg mixture.

Mix well and chill.

Form into 1-inch balls and roll in granulated sugar to coat.

Place on a cookie sheet 2 inches apart.

Bake at 375° F for 8-10 minutes.

Mom's Soft Raisin Cookies: Submitted by Cindy Lawyer. This recipe belonged to Ardella Wiesner.

Soak 1 box of raisins in hot water until soft, set aside

Mix the following:

2 cups of sugar
1 cup Crisco
1 cup milk
1 teaspoon baking powder
1 teaspoon baking soda
½ teaspoon salt
1 teaspoon vanilla
3 eggs
4 ½ cups flour
*Optional: oats and or nuts

Drain raisins and fold them into the batter.

*You can add oats and nuts if desired.

Bake at 350° F for 14- 15 minutes.

Pumpkin Cookies: Submitted by Brenda Wylie

Ingredients:

3 cups granulated sugar
1 ½ cup shortening
1 large can (solid pack) pumpkin
5 cups flour
3 teaspoons baking powder
3 teaspoons soda
3 teaspoons vanilla
3 teaspoons cinnamon
1- 16-ounce bag chocolate chips
1 cup chopped nuts
½ box raisins

Instructions:

Beat the following ingredients together: Granulated sugar, cup shortening, pumpkin, flour, baking powder, soda, vanilla, and cinnamon.

Then add chocolate chips, chopped nuts, and raisins.

Bake on greased cookie sheets between 350° F - 375° F for 12 minutes.

Makes about 6-7 dozen.

Grandma Gruver's Old-Fashioned Sand Tarts:

Submitted by Cindy Lawyer

Ingredients:

2 cups sugar
1 cup butter
3 eggs
3 cups flour
1 teaspoon baking powder

Instructions:

Cream together sugar, butter, and eggs.

Sift together flour and baking soda.

Add flour mixture a handful at a time working it until it's stiff enough to roll.

Cut into shapes with cookie cutters.

Brush with egg whites.

Sprinkle them with sugar and cinnamon.

Bake at 375° F for 10-15 minutes or light golden brown.

Moravian Sand Tart Cookies: Submitted by Eileen Bink. This recipe belonged to her grandmother, Amanda Myers.

Ingredients for cookie:

2 cups butter
1 teaspoon vanilla extract
2 ½ cups confectioners' sugar (10X sugar)
5 eggs
4 cups sifted flour
1 teaspoon baking soda

*If you want thicker cookies, add ½-1 teaspoon baking powder

Ingredients for topping:

1 beaten egg white
Cinnamon sugar (eyeball amount)
Walnut or pecan halves (eyeball amount)

Instructions:

Cream together butter and vanilla. Add sugar gradually, creaming until fluffy.

Add eggs one at a time, beating well after each addition until blended.

Chill dough overnight.

Using a small amount of dough at a time, roll out on a floured surface. The dough will be sticky.

Cut out with cookie cutters. Place into an ungreased baking sheet. Brush with egg white and sprinkle with cinnamon sugar. Top with nuts.

Bake at 350°F for 10-13 minutes.

Aunt June's Snickerdoodle: Submitted by Eileen Bink

Ingredients for cookie:

½ cup margarine
2 eggs
½ cup Crisco
½ teaspoon salt
1 ½ cup sugar
1 teaspoon baking soda
2 teaspoons cream of tartar
2 ¾ cups sifted flour

Cream together both the shortening and sugar. Add eggs and beat well.

Sift together flour, soda, cream of tartar, and salt. Combine flour mixture with the cream mixture.

Chill dough.

Roll chilled dough into small walnut-sized balls. Roll each ball into the topping mixture.

Ingredients for topping:

4 tablespoons sugar
4 teaspoons cinnamon

Place coated balls onto an ungreased baking sheet.

Bake at 400°F for 8-10 minutes or until golden brown, but still soft.

Raspberry Custard: Submitted by Cindy Lawyer. This recipe belonged to her grandma, Isabella Gruver.

Ingredients:

3 eggs
3 tablespoons sugar
½ teaspoon cornstarch
1 ¾ cups milk
1 quart of raspberries

Instructions:

Mix and pour into a pie shell.

Add a quart of raspberries, enough to fill the entire top. They will float.

Bake 400° F for 35-40 min.

Raspberry Custard with Bisquick:

Ingredients:

1 cup Bisquick
2 eggs
3 tablespoons sugar
1 ¾ cups milk
1 quart of raspberries

Instructions:

Mix and pour into a pie shell. Add a quart of raspberries.

Bake at 400° F for 35-40 min.

Grandma Gruver's Pie Crust: Submitted by Cindy Lawyer

Makes one 9-inch shell

Ingredients:

2 cups sifted flour
⅔ cup shortening
1 teaspoon salt
5-7 tablespoons cold water

Instructions:

Cut shortening into sifted flour and salt to pea-sized pieces.

Add enough water to hold the mixture together.

Divide and roll out on a floured board.

Strawberry Pie: Submitted by Gloria Apple

Ingredients:

1 can of soda (Sprite, 7Up, Ginger Ale)
1 small box of strawberry Jell-O
2 tablespoons cornstarch + ¼ cup of water
2 cups of strawberries, sliced
Graham Cracker crust (store-bought)

Instructions:

In a saucepan, whisk soda and Jell-O together.

Add cornstarch and water mixture. Cook, stirring until clear. Remove from heat and cool.

Chill for several hours before serving.

Jiffy Cherry Pie: Submitted by Melinda Gochenaur. This recipe belonged to Mrs. Wm. Herman, Jr.

Ingredients for pie:

1 can of sour cherries
1 cup sugar
2 tablespoons cornstarch
Pinch of salt
1 baked 8-inch pie shell

Ingredients for butter crumbs:

½ cup flour
¼ cup sugar
2 tablespoons butter
Pinch of salt

Instructions:

Mix cherries with sugar, cornstarch, and salt; cook until thick.

Pour into baked pie shell.

Top with crumbs and brown under the broiler.

Sour Cream Raisin Pie: Submitted by Nannie Fish. This recipe belonged to her grandmother, Celia Knudsen Beshore.

Ingredients:

1 16 oz container of sour cream
1 cup sugar
3 egg yolks, save whites for meringue
1 teaspoon cinnamon
Pinch of salt
1 cup raisins
1 8-inch pie shell

Instructions:

Bake at 350° F

Top with meringue. Bake for 6- 10 minutes.

Lemon Sponge Pie: Submitted by Kyle Beissel. This recipe belongs to Emma Steffy and Katie Heilman.

Ingredients:

1 lemon, grated, and juiced
1 tablespoon margarine
1 cup milk
2 egg whites
2 egg yolks
2 tablespoons flour
1 cup of sugar

Instructions:

Mix sugar and margarine to make it creamy.

Add flour, lemon rind, lemon juice, egg yolks, and milk.

In another bowl beat egg whites until stiff, then fold them into the other mixture.

Pour into 1 9-inch unbaked pie crust.

Bake at 400° F for 5 minutes and 350° F until done at 45-50 minutes.

Montgomery Pie:
Montgomery Pie: Submitted by Kyle Beissel. This recipe belongs to Katie Heilman and Doris Pugh.

Ingredients:

Top-
2 eggs
½ cups shortening
2 cups sugar
2 cups flour
1 teaspoon baking soda in 1 cup sour milk or 2 teaspoons baking powder in 1 cup sweet milk

Bottom-
1 lemon, grated and juiced
½ cup hot water

Instructions:

Mix the bottom ingredients and pour into an unbaked 9-inch pie crust.

Mix the top ingredients and place them on top of the other mixture.

Bake at 350° F for 30 minutes.

No-Bake Fresh Peach Pie: Submitted by Gloria Apple

Ingredients:

1 cup sugar
1 3-ounce package of peach Jell-O (½ cup)
2 tablespoons cornstarch
1 cup boiling water
3 ½- 4 cups fresh peaches, sliced, skin removed
Pie crust, store-bought (or vanilla wafers)
Cool Whip topping

Instructions:

Mix sugar, Jell-O, and cornstarch. Add boiling water. Continue to boil for 2 minutes (or until clear and thick).

Layer peaches in a Graham Cracker crust, on top of a vanilla wafer, or a prebaked pie shell.

Refrigerate. Add Cool Whip topping.

Serve cold.

Éclair Cake: Submitted by Kathy Witten

Ingredients:

1 box graham crackers
2 small boxes of French Vanilla Instant Pudding
12 ounces Cool Whip (defrosted in the refrigerator)
3 ½ cups milk
1 tub of dark chocolate frosting

Instructions:

Butter the bottom and sides of a 9x13 inch pan.

Mix pudding and milk. Fold in Cool Whip.

Place a layer of graham crackers on the bottom of the pan to cover the bottom.

Spread half of the pudding/Cool Whip mixture on top of the graham cracker layer.

Place the second layer of graham crackers on top of the pudding.

Spread the remaining pudding/Cool Whip mixture over the second layer of graham crackers.

Cover with a final layer of graham crackers. Microwave frosting for 20-30 seconds to soften (or make your own dark chocolate frosting).

Spread warmed frosting over the graham crackers.

Refrigerate at least overnight. (This softens the graham crackers)

Salad Dressing Cake: Submitted by Susan Rudy. This recipe belonged to her mom.

Ingredients:

2 cups flour
1 cup sugar
1 cup salad dressing
1 cup water
6 tablespoons cocoa
1 teaspoon vanilla
2 teaspoons baking soda

Instructions:

Mix the dry ingredients first.

Bake at 350- 374°F

Black Forrest Cherry Cake: Submitted by Nancy Ickes

Ingredients for cake:

1 cup butter
2 cup sugar
4 eggs
2 cups sifted all-purpose flour
½ teaspoon salt
1 ½ teaspoon baking soda
⅔ cup buttermilk
1 teaspoon vanilla
3 oz unsweetened chocolate, grated

Instructions for the cake:

Preheat oven to 325° F.

Grease and flour three 9-inch cake pans.

Cream the butter and sugar. Add eggs one at a time and beat well after each edition. After the last egg is added, beat 1 minute or until the mixture is light and fluffy.

Sift flour with salt. Mix baking soda with the buttermilk and add alternately with flour to the creamed mixture.

Add vanilla. Melt the chocolate in ⅔ cup boiling water, stir until smooth. Blend chocolate into the cake mixture.

Pour into prepared pans and bake for 30 to 35 minutes, or until cake tests done.

Ingredients for filling:

1 can (17 oz) pitted dark sweet cherries
2 tablespoons cornstarch
¼ cup water

The recipe is continued on next page...

Instructions for the filling:

Drain liquid from the cherries into saucepan, reserve cherries.

Bring liquid to a boil. Mix cornstarch with ¼ cup water and stir into juice. Cook until clear. Add cherries; cool (do not chill).

Ingredients for chocolate buttercream frosting:

4 tablespoons butter
1 large egg white (or 2 small egg whites), unbeaten
3 oz semi-sweet chocolate, melted
2 cups sifted confectioner's sugar
1 teaspoon vanilla

Instructions for chocolate buttercream frosting:

Cream butter, add sugar, egg whites, and vanilla.

Add chocolate and continue beating until smooth.

Ingredients for whipped cream icing:

4 packages (2 boxes) Dream Whip (prepare using instructions on the box, reducing milk by ¼ cup)
⅓ cup Kirsch (Kirschwasser from the liquor store {this is a type of cherry brandy, but do not substitute other cherry brandy for Kirschwasser})

Instructions for whipped cream icing:

Whip the cream whip until soft peaks are formed.

Pour in ¼ cup of Kirsch, a little at a time, beating only until the cream takes it up. Reserve the rest of the Kirschwasser.

The recipe is continued on next page…

Assembling the cake:

Place one layer of cake on a large cake plate.

Spread the chocolate buttercream frosting along the edge of the bottom layer, forming a ring on the layer. This should leave an empty circle inside the ring. Fill the circle with cherries.

Prick top all over with a fork. Sprinkle lightly with reserved Kirsch (can use more Kirsch if you want). Spread the layer with 1 inch of Dream Whip.

Put the top layer on gently. Spread sides and top with remaining Dream Whip.

Garnish top with chocolate curls or grated chocolate from a semi-sweet chocolate bar. Dot with Maraschino cherries. "I think it works best with cherries cut in half drained on a paper towel".

Refrigerate until serving time.

Ardella's Zucchini Bread: Submitted by Cindy Lawyer. This recipe belonged to Ardella Wiesner.

Mix:

3 eggs, lightly beaten
1 cup oil
1 ½ cups sugar
2 cups zucchini, grated
2 teaspoons vanilla

Mix:

2 cups flour
½ teaspoons baking powder
2 teaspoons baking soda
3 teaspoons cinnamon
1 teaspoon salt

Add to the wet mixture. Mix well.

Add:

1 cup raisins and 1 cup chopped nuts.

Bake at 350° F for 55- 60 minutes in a greased and floured loaf pan.

Homemade Ice Cream: Submitted by Nancy Ickes. This recipe belonged to her mom, Mary Brenneman Heilman.

Ingredients:

2 cups sugar
4 eggs
1-quart whole milk
1 pt cream
1 teaspoon vanilla
1 teaspoon Butter and Nut Vanilla

Instructions:

Mix sugar and eggs with an electric beater in a large mixing bowl. Add cream, vanilla, and Butter and Nut Vanilla; add milk, beat gently.

Pour into an electric freezer canister. Follow directions for freezing. When finished, serve immediately or put into the freezer compartment of the refrigerator.

Makes about ½ gallon.

Scissor Candy: Submitted by Diane Garman. This recipe belonged to her grandmother, Kathryn Fidler Shaffer.

Ingredients:

3 cups sugar
1 cup white Karo
1 cup water
1 teaspoon flavored oil (cinnamon, mint, clove, etc) or extract
Food coloring

Instructions:

Cook until the candy thermometer reaches 310° F (hard crack).

Color may be added during cooking.

Remove from heat - add flavored oil.

Pour into a greased jelly roll pan.

Cut with scissors when cool enough to handle, but still quite hot.

*Powder with cornstarch if desired.

Recipe yields 1 pound of candy

Flitch: Submitted by Diane Garman. This recipe belonged to her grandmother, Kathryn Fidler Shaffer.

Ingredients:

4 teaspoons instant nonfat milk
4 teaspoons instant mashed potatoes
4 tablespoons hot water
4 cups powdered sugar
Creamy peanut butter
*Optional: semi-sweet chocolate

Instructions:

Mix instant nonfat milk, and instant mashed potatoes, beat in hot water.

Add powdered sugar, mix until firm.

Roll very thin, spread with a thin layer of peanut butter.

Roll up and slice into 1-inch pieces.

*May dip in semi-sweet chocolate.

Rock Cake: Submitted by Diane Garman. This recipe belonged to her mother-in-law, Ellen Wilt Garman.

Ingredients:

2 cups brown sugar
1 cup butter or margarine
3 eggs
3 cups flour
1 teaspoon cinnamon
1 teaspoon baking soda in ⅓ cup hot water
1-pound raisins
½ pound dates
½ pound nuts
½ teaspoon salt

Instructions:

Place flour in a bowl, rub in the butter. Should resemble breadcrumbs.

Stir in sugar, spice, fruits, and nuts.

Beat eggs and add water to which baking soda has been dissolved. Mix into dry ingredients and form a stiff dough.

Place in small, rough heaps on a greased cookie sheet.

Bake at 400° F for 15 minutes or until golden brown.

Spice Pudding: Submitted by Lana Fink

Ingredients for batter:

1 cup sugar
1 cup flour
½ cup milk
4 tablespoons butter
2 teaspoons baking powder
2 teaspoons cinnamon

Instructions for batter:

Mix all together.

Ingredients for syrup:

2 cups water
4 tablespoons butter
1 cup brown sugar (packed)

Instructions for syrup:

Mix syrup ingredients in a saucepan and heat to dissolve sugar.

DO NOT BOIL

Pour into a 9x9 inch pan and spoon batter into syrup.

Bake at 350° F for 40 minutes. Serve warm or cold with whipped topping or vanilla ice cream.

Creamy Rice Pudding: Submitted by Donna Smith

Ingredients:

1-quart milk
4 tablespoons rice
4 eggs, separated
2 tablespoons sugar
Pinch of salt
Cinnamon (to taste)

Instructions:

Boil milk, rice, and salt until the rice is done.

Beat egg yolks, and the sugar together. Add mixture to milk and rice. Let Cool.

Beat egg whites and gradually add 4 tablespoons of sugar.

Fold the egg white sugar mixture with the milk rice mixture. Sprinkle with cinnamon.

Chill.

Cherry Pudding: Submitted by Donna Smith

"This recipe is 90 years old, at least. My Mother is 85 years old, and the recipe was given to her by her mother-in-law."

Ingredients:

3/4 cup sugar
1 egg
1 teaspoon butter
1/2 cup milk
1 ½ cups flour
1 teaspoon baking powder
1-pint cherries

Instructions:

Pour mixture into a buttered and floured cake pan.

Bake at 350°F degrees for 25 to 30 minutes.

Shoo-fly Pie: Submitted by Brenda Fludovich

Ingredients for the liquid part:

½ cup molasses
½ cup hot water
½ teaspoon baking soda

Ingredients for the crumb part:

¼ cup shortening
1 cup brown sugar
1 ½ cups flour
¼ teaspoon salt
1 teaspoon cinnamon
A little nutmeg, ginger, and cloves

Instructions:

Combine the dry ingredients and work in the shortening to make crumbs.

Into an unbaked pie shell put a layer of crumbs. Then layer liquid and crumbs, ending with crumbs on the top.

Bake in a hot oven at 450° F for 15 minutes, then reduce heat to 350° F for 20 minutes.

Egg Custard: Submitted by Brenda Fludovich

Ingredients:

3 eggs
2 cups scalded milk
⅓ cup sugar
Dash of nutmeg
Dash of salt
Vanilla

Instructions:

Mix all ingredients and pour into a pie pan.

Bake at 420° F for 12- 15 minutes.

Then at 300° F for 25- 30 minutes.

Orange Delight: Submitted by Gloria Hoover

Ingredients:

2 packs of orange Jell-O
2 cups hot water
1 cup cold water
2 cups crushed pineapple
1 large bowl of Cool Whip

Instructions:

Beat Jell-O, pineapple, and water together.

Let chill slightly.

Beat in the Cool Whip.

Put in the refrigerator until jelled and ready to serve.

Applesauce Cheese Swirl: Submitted by Donna Smith

Dissolve and chill:

2 3oz packets of lemon Jell-O
1/2 cup cinnamon red candies

Mix:

2 cups applesauce
1 tablespoon lemon juice
Dash of salt

Swirl through Applesauce Mixture:

2 3oz Cream Cheese
¼ cup milk
2 tablespoons salad dressing

Mom's Cherry Pudding: Submitted by Lou Ann Horvath Kauffman

Ingredients:

2 cups sugar

¼ cup shortening (margarine or Crisco)

2 eggs

1 cup milk

½ teaspoon salt

3 teaspoons baking powder

4 cups flour *Some of the flour can be used to coat the cherries.

3 cups sour cherries (can use more)

Instructions:

Coat cherries in flour. Set aside.

Mix all other ingredients. The batter will be stiff.

Add cherries to batter.

Pour into a greased and floured 9 x 13-inch pan.

Bake at 350° F for 45 minutes.

Pumpkin Bread: Submitted by Gail Miller

Ingredients:

3 ½ cups flour
2 teaspoons baking soda
1 teaspoon salt
2 teaspoons cinnamon
3 cups sugar
1 cup oil
4 eggs
⅔ cup water
2 cups pumpkin (Libby's canned pumpkin)
Handful of raisins

Instructions:

Mix ingredients with an electric mixer.

Separate batter into 3 loaf pans.

Bake at 350° F for 1 hour.

Pumpkin Bread: Submitted by Gina Mickle Reever. This recipe belonged to her grandmother, Loretta Harlacher, née Mikos.

Ingredients:

3 cups sugar
4 eggs
2 sticks melted margarine
2/3 cup warm water
2 cups pumpkin
1 teaspoon vanilla
1 ½ teaspoons salt
1 teaspoon nutmeg
1 teaspoon cinnamon
2 teaspoons baking soda
3 ½ cups flour
1 cup chopped walnuts
4- 1 pound metal coffee cans (empty)

Instructions:

Mix all ingredients in the order listed above with an electric mixer.

Grease the inside of four- 1 pound metal coffee cans and fill half full with batter.

Preheat the oven to 350° F and bake for 1 hour or until it is not wet on top.

Remove from the oven and allow the loaves to remain in the cans for 10 minutes, then take out of the cans and cool on racks.

Refrigerate in Ziplock bags after completely cool.

Apple Rolls: Submitted by Kyle Beissel. This recipe belongs to Shirley Wilt.

Ingredients:

4 medium apples, peeled and cut fine
1 ½ cup brown sugar
1 tablespoon of margarine
1 tablespoon sugar
2 cups water
1 tablespoon cinnamon
¾ cup milk
6 tablespoons shortening
4 teaspoons baking powder

Instructions:

Peel, core apples, and chop fine. Set them aside.

Put sugar and water in a 13x9 greased baking pan on the stove for 5 minutes.

Mix dough and roll ¼ inch thick in a rectangular shape.

Spread butter on the rolled dough, then add sugar and cinnamon mixture. Add apples.

Roll like a jelly roll.

Slice 1 inch thick and lay in sugar water, in the pan.

Bake at 350°F for 30 minutes. As they cool, the broth becomes thicker. Eat warm or cold.

Cornstarch Pudding: Submitted by Gail Miller

Ingredients:

⅓ cup sugar
¼ cup cornstarch
⅛ teaspoon salt
2 ¾ cups milk
2 tablespoons butter
1 teaspoon vanilla

Instructions:

Mix sugar, cornstarch, and salt in a saucepan.

Stir in milk and bring to a boil. Cook for 1 minute.

Remove from heat.

Stir in butter and vanilla.

Pour into bowls, cover, and refrigerate.

Peanut Butter Pie: Submitted by JoAnn Seker

Ingredients:

8 ounces cream cheese
1 cup powdered sugar
½ cup creamy peanut butter
16 ounces Cool Whip (divided)
Hot fudge sauce
Graham cracker pie crust (recipe below or buy store-bought)
Reese's Peanut Butter Cups, chopped (optional)

Instructions:

Take the cooled graham cracker pie crust and spoon hot fudge sauce from the jar onto the bottom of the crust to cover (make this as thick or as thin as you want it).

In a large bowl, mix the cream cheese, powdered sugar, peanut butter, and 8-ounces of Cool Whip.

Pour onto the pie crust.

Top with the rest of the Cool Whip.

Sprinkle with the chopped Reese's Peanut Butter Cups.

Graham Cracker Pie Crust Ingredients:

¼ cups graham cracker crumbs
2 tablespoons sugar
3 cups melted butter

Graham Cracker Pie Crust Instructions:

Mix the three ingredients until thoroughly blended. Pack mixture on the bottom and sides of a 9-inch pie pan. Bake at 350° F for 8 minutes.

Wacky Cake: Submitted by JoAnn Seker

Ingredients:

3 cups flour
2 cups sugar
6 tablespoons cocoa
2 tablespoons baking soda
1 teaspoon salt
2 teaspoons vanilla
2 teaspoons vinegar
10 tablespoons vegetable oil
2 cups cold water

Instructions:

Mix ingredients.

Pour into a 13 x 9-inch pan.

Bake at 250° F for 40-45 minutes.

Scripture Cake: Submitted by Kyle Beissel. This recipe belongs to Bevelery Botterbusch.

Ingredients:

1 cup butter   *Judges 5:25*
1 cup water   *Genesis 24:11*
2 cups sugar   *Jeremiah 6:20*
6 eggs   *Isaiah 10:14*
3 cups flour   *I Kings 4:22*
1 teaspoon salt   *Leviticus 2:13*
2 cups raisins   *I Samuel 25:18*
1 teaspoon honey   *Exodus 16:31*
2 cups figs   *I Samuel 25:18*
Sweet spices   *I King 10:2*
1 cup almonds   *Genesis 43:11*
2 teaspoons baking powder   *I Corinthians 5:6*

Behold! There was a cake baked! *I Kings 19:6*

Instructions:

Stir and mix all ingredients.

Proverbs 23:14 You will have made a good cake!

Pumpkin Custard Pie: Submitted by Gina Mickle Reever. This recipe belonged to her grandmother, Loretta Harlacher, née Mikos.

Ingredients for Pumpkin Custard:

2 cups fresh pumpkin
¾ to 1 cup granulated sugar
2 -3 eggs
1 teaspoon vanilla
1 cup whole milk

Instructions:

Mix all ingredients with an electric mixer. Pour into a 9-inch pie crust. (See pie crust instructions below)

Sprinkle with cinnamon.

Bake at 425° F for 12 minutes. Then reduce temperature to 350° F and bake for another 35 to 40 minutes.

The pie is done when a knife inserted in the center comes out clean.

Single Pie Crust Ingredients:

1 ⅓ cups flour
½ teaspoon salt
Scant ½ cup Crisco
3 tablespoons water

Single Pie Crust Instructions:

Stir the salt and flour together, then add Crisco and work together with your fingers until it gets crumbly.
Add the water and cut together with a butter knife or pastry cutter. If it's too wet add a little more flour.

Cranberry Jell-O Mold: Submitted by Rosie Coligan Helbus

Ingredients:

2 cups water
2 cups sugar
4 cups fresh cranberries
2 - 3 ounce packages of strawberry Jell-O
16-ounce crushed pineapples, drained
*1 cup chopped walnuts, optional

Instructions:

Bring water, sugar, and cranberries to a boil. Boil till all berries pop.

Remove from heat.

Add Jell-O and stir until dissolved.

Add pineapple and nuts.

Stir till mixed.

Pour into your favorite mold.

Chill.

Cherry/Raspberry Pudding: Submitted by Candice Conley. This recipe belonged to her mother, Janette Gross Lowery.

Ingredients:

1-2 cups fruit, cherries, or raspberries
1 ¾ cups flour
2 ½ teaspoons baking powder
½ teaspoon salt
¼ cup margarine
1 cup sugar
1 egg
1 teaspoon vanilla
⅔ cup milk

Instructions:

Grease and flour an 8-inch square pan.

Mix all ingredients and pour into the baking pan.

Bake at 350° F for 45- 60 minutes.

Check for doneness with a toothpick.

Academic Bowl Cake: Submitted by Judi Bourque

*This was a favorite of the students who participated on the Fishing Creek Elementary School's 4th and 5th Grade Academic Bowl teams. I coached the teams for a few years and the students came to expect this cake during competition break times.

Chocolate Cake Ingredients:

1 box of chocolate cake mix
1 small box of chocolate <u>instant</u> pudding
4 eggs
¼ cup oil
¾ cup water

Chocolate Cake Instructions:

Use an electric mixer and mix all ingredients on medium/high for 6-8 minutes. Put into a greased Bundt cake pan. Bake at 350° F for 40-45 minutes. (I usually take the cake out when it starts to pull away from the sides of the pan).

Yellow Cake:

Use Yellow cake, a small box of vanilla instant pudding, 1 teaspoon vanilla, 4 eggs, ¼ cup oil, ¾ cup water. Follow the same directions as chocolate cake.

Frosting Ingredients:

1 pound of 10X sugar (confectioners)
1 stick of butter
1 teaspoon vanilla
Enough milk to make spreading consistency

Frosting Instructions:
If you want chocolate frosting- add ¼ cup of Hershey's cocoa

Candied Pecans: Submitted by Kathy Witten

Ingredients:

1 cup white sugar
1 teaspoon ground cinnamon
1 teaspoon salt
1 egg white
1 tablespoon water
1 pound pecan halves

Instructions:

Preheat the oven to 250° F (120° C).

Mix sugar, cinnamon, and salt together in a bowl.

Whisk egg white and water together in a separate bowl until frothy.

Toss pecans in the egg white mixture.

Mix sugar mixture into pecan mixture until pecans are evenly coated.

Spread coated pecans onto a baking sheet.

Bake, stirring every 15 minutes until pecans are evenly browned, 1 hour.

Beverages

bev·er·age
/ˈbev(ə)rij/
Noun

A drink, especially one other than water.

Dandelion Wine: Submitted by Diane Garman. This recipe belonged to her mother-in-law, Ellen Wilt Garman.

Ingredients:

4 quarts dandelion flowers
4 quarts boiling water
4 pounds sugar
3 lemons, sliced
3 yeast cakes

Instructions:

Mix dandelion flowers into boiling water.

Let stand for 24 hours. Then separate out the solids.

Add sugar, lemons, and yeast cakes.

Let mixture stand for 10 days before separating out solids and putting the liquid mixture into a jug.

Dandelion Wine: Submitted by Kyle Beissel. This recipe belonged to Homer Beard.

Ingredients:

3 or 4 quarts of dandelion yellow blossoms
2 ½ pounds of sugar
2 lemons, sliced
3 oranges, sliced
½ yeast cake

Instructions:

Scald dandelion blossoms in hot water. Leave to stand for 24 hours.

Add other ingredients, dissolve yeast cake in lukewarm water. Lease to stand for about 2 weeks.

It should be ready for drinking after 2 weeks. If not drank, put into a gallon crock or glass jugs with a cork on top.

Pennsylvania Bolio: Submitted by Dominish Miller

Ingredients:

2 liters of ginger ale
6 cinnamon sticks
1 teaspoon caraway seeds
10 cloves
1 tablespoon peppercorns
1 tablespoon allspice
3 oranges, sliced
2 lemons, sliced
½ cup raisins
2 pounds of honey
1 bottle of your favorite whiskey

Instructions:

Start to heat the ginger ale in a large pot.

Add sliced fruit and other ingredients to ginger ale.

Bring mixture to a boil.

Remove from heat and strain.

Add whiskey.

Serve warm.

Chocolate Cream: Submitted by Dominish Miller

Ingredients:

1 cup water
5 ounces milk chocolate, grated
1 cup sugar
4 cups heavy whipping cream

Instructions:

Melt the grated chocolate over a double boiler.

Blend in sugar and 1 cup of the heavy whipping cream until the mixture is smooth.

Move chocolate into a saucepan and add the remaining heavy whipping cream.

Stir the mixture until scalding.

Serve warm.

Optional- Whisk some chocolate into a froth and spoon on top when serving.

Irish Cream: Submitted by Debbie Sorenson

Ingredients:

1 3/4 Cups Jameson Irish Whiskey

4 eggs

2 teaspoons instant coffee

1 14 oz can sweetened condensed milk

2 tablespoons Hershey's chocolate syrup

1 teaspoon pure vanilla extract

½ teaspoon almond extract

Instructions:

Add all the ingredients to a blender and combine for 1-2 minutes.

Pour into a glass airtight container and refrigerate for up to 6 weeks.